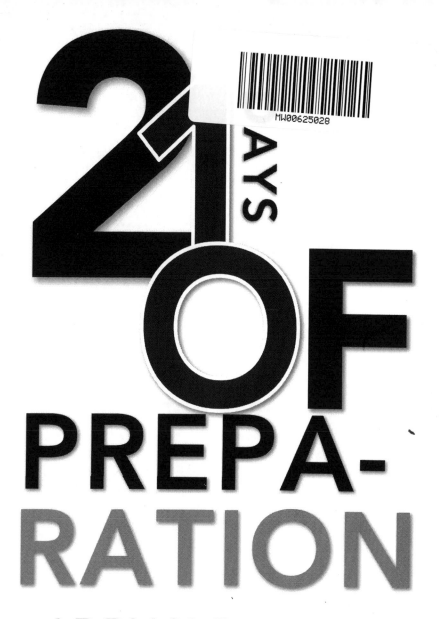

# 21 DAYS OF PREPA-RATION

## ADRIAN D. DAVIS

KEEN VISION PUBLISHING

**Limits of Liability and Disclaimer of Warranty**

The author and publisher shall not be liable for your
misuse of this material. This book is strictly for
informational and educational purposes. The purpose
of this book is to educate and entertain. The author
and/or publisher do not guarantee that anyone
following these techniques, suggestions, tips, ideas, or
strategies will become successful. The author and/or
publisher shall have neither liability nor responsibility
to anyone with respect to any loss or damage caused,
or alleged to be caused, directly or indirectly by the
information contained in this book.

Views expressed in this publication do not necessarily
reflect the views of the publisher.
Printed in the United States of America

ISBN 978-0-9987200-7-4
Keen Vision Publishing, LLC
www.keen-vision.com

# ACKNOWLEDGEMENTS

This book is dedicated to my brother and best friend, Pastor Christopher Sands. During the loss of his sister, I witnessed Chris jump into a role he did not foresee, but had intentionally prepared for. Over the course of our friendship, I have watched Chris prepare for the position he is in now. Though he did not know how he would enter the role of being a full-time father to his nieces & nephews and a vital leader of the youth of Chattanooga, TN, he walked into the position ready because of all the work he had put in over the years. Chris, Mama Candis, Serenity, Christion, Cameron, & Trinity, I love you guys! I commend you all for how you have pressed through during the unexpected. I love you guys!

I would like to acknowledge my parents, Priscilla McGhee and Anthony Davis; my step-father, Harold McGhee; my step-mother, Sue Davis; and my sister, Camille. Finally, I would like to express my love and appreciation to the amazing group of people I've been honored with the responsibility of leading, All Nations Worship Assembly - Huntsville, AL.

# ABOUT THE AUTHOR

Pastor Adrian D. Davis is a native of Chattanooga, Tennessee. He currently serves as the Senior Pastor of All Nations Worship Assembly in Huntsville, Alabama. This man of God delivers messages of hope, positivity, and empowerment that are sustaining and motivating to individuals across the world. His motto, "It's better to train up whole children than to fix broken adults," encourages us to reach back and help the next generation who will carry us forward.

Pastor AD has served in several ministries throughout the southeast as a Youth Pastor. He received his Master's degree in Divinity from Johnson Bible College In Nashville, Tennessee. Pastor AD is one-half of the world-renowned duo known as Beyond Words Mime Ministry. Through this mime ministry, he has traveled the world leading souls to Christ for over ten years.

Pastor AD accepted his call into the ministry at the young age of 18, and he has blossomed into a powerful man of God who knows and understands his call and passion to see our youth accept Christ as their personal Lord and Savior. Pastor AD is a trailblazer amongst the new breed of ministers who embrace the "young believers". He has single handedly broken the stereotype of yesterday's clergyman in the Huntsville community and is equipping the new generation to not only learn, but serve, and most importantly grow.

Most known for his nontraditional approach to the word of God, Pastor AD paints vivid pictures of the Gospel and illustrates the text by getting God's people involved. He creates interactive ways of preaching the Word without changing God's message. He serves as a "pastor to pastors", social activist for change, motivational speaker, mentor to hundreds of high school and college students in the Tennessee Valley area, community developer, and most recently "Best Selling Author" for his first book, Tears Down a Smiling Face, released November 12, 2013.

Pastor AD acknowledges that the Lord has sent him on a mission to teach, translate, transform, and train his people.

# CONTENTS

# INTRODUCTION

A s human beings, we naturally want better. Each of us possesses an inner desire to advance beyond where we are now. Though our culture, age, or socio-economic status may cause our desired areas of improvement to differ, everyone desires to be better, have better, or feel better about some area of their lives.

During my visit to Ghana, I met some of the most amazing children. They lived in an impoverished area and were grateful for things we often overlook like clean water, rice, and dry floors. Even though they were very grateful for any little thing they received, they still had an inner desire to see their lives improve.

Each of us was born with an unsettling natural desire for advancement. Just look at an infant anywhere between six months to a year. Though they may not be able to walk yet, their inability to walk does not prevent them from attempting to move around. They kick their legs, find things to hold themselves up, scoot, crawl, etc. They do whatever they can to be mobile until they can stand and walk.

At this point, you may have the same question I've pondered for years: If we all desire to be better, why aren't we all better? James 2:17 tells us that faith without works is dead. The reason many of us are not yet where we desire to be is that we are operating with

a dead faith. James 2:17 tells us three major things about faith:
1. Faith should be living.
2. Work brings faith to life.
3. Dead faith won't accomplish anything.

The word faith is defined as having complete trust or confidence in something or someone. Hebrews 11:1 tells us that faith is the substance of things hoped for and the evidence of things not seen. Faith is the base of our salvation and is required for every area of our lives. Without faith, we are hopeless. The concept of faith is quite easy to understand. Believe it or not, we exercise faith daily. For instance, when we walk into a building, we have faith that it won't collapse. We use stairs confidently without ever suspecting that they could crumble beneath us. When we go into a restaurant, we have faith that the food we are eating won't make us sick. Many of us find it easy to have faith in man-made things, but struggle to have faith in the promises of God. Our lack of faith in God is evident in how we prepare for what He has promised us. James explains to us in James 2:17 that we can have all the faith we want, but if it is not accompanied by work, then that faith is dead. At some point, we must ask ourselves: Do I have enough faith in God to work towards what He promised?

Here's the issue. We know that God *can* make good on His promises, but deep down inside, we don't believe He *will* do it for us. We've heard the testimonies of others. We've read about instances in the Bible where the faith of an individual caused them to be healed. We've seen God do the miraculous for those around us, but we don't believe that He *WILL* do the same for us. Since we don't believe that He will come through for us, we don't see a need to work towards His promises.

For many of us, we feel as though we've screwed up too many opportunities to see the goodness of God manifest in our lives, but this is not so. Scripture tells us that His grace and mercy are new each day. In Psalm 23, David decreed that goodness and mercy would follow him all the days of his life. If you know anything about David, you know he was far from perfect, and far from deserving of God's goodness and mercy. However, David still experienced it. God didn't do this for David because David was perfect. He did it because David believed that He would! Rest assured that you are not alone in your slip-ups and bad decisions. We've all fallen short, but we must make the decision not to stay there. We must accept God's forgiveness, and forgive ourselves. God is a Redeemer and a Restorer. I don't care how much you've messed up, your mess is never greater than God's redeeming and restoring power. Old things have passed away. Today is a new day. Choose to prepare for what God has promised you despite what your past may say. You must believe and stand on the fact that God *can* do it, and He WILL do it for YOU!

Many of you reading this book have found yourself in a place of stagnation. You feel like something great is on the horizon, however, you've grown impatient in waiting for it. You've been spinning your wheels and doing all you know to do, but it seems as though you just can't break out of where you are. You've been praying, dispatching angels, fasting, decreeing, and declaring, but it doesn't seem like anything is happening for you. For the next 21 days, let's challenge ourselves to put our work where our faith is and prepare for what we have been asking God for. Desiring something is easy, however, preparing for it requires intentionality and consistency. Instead of just decreeing, declaring, and prophesying over ourselves, we must also get our hands dirty and work toward what we believe in.

So, what does faith work look like? When we work towards the things we are believing God for, we intentionally take the necessary steps to prepare for what we do not see. Often, when we think about taking faith steps, our minds instantly begin to consider the "big moves", like completing the application, making the phone call, putting in the request, etc. As a result, we overlook the major actions of faith, like preparing mentally and spiritually for what we are anticipating. Over the next 21 days, we will focus on areas of our lives we tend to look over as we prepare for our next. As we journey from day to day, open your mind and heart to receive the information you read. Allow it to change your life for the rest of your life. Before we begin, let's pray:

*Most Gracious God,*

*I lift to you the individual reading this book. I thank you for their life. I give you glory for the purpose you've placed on the inside of them. For the next twenty-one days, allow them to hear you. I command the scales to fall from their eyes, in the name of Jesus. I decree and declare that they will be disciplined in their preparation for what you are doing in their life. In Jesus' Name, Amen.*

DAY ONE

# YOU HAVE BEEN
# SELECTED

*"But you are not like that, for you are a chosen people. You are royal priests, a holy nation, God's very own possession. As a result, you can show others the goodness of God, for he called you out of the darkness into his wonderful light." 1 Peter 2:9 (NLT)*

From time to time, we find ourselves second guessing what God has called us to do. We look at life with our natural eyes and weigh-in our mistakes, shortcomings, past decisions, generational curses, and finances. With so much against us, we feel like there's no way God could have called us to do anything. Here's what we must keep in the forefront of our minds: When God selected us for the vision, He was well-aware of what we would be born into, the mistakes we would make, and the dumb things we would do. Despite all of this, He still chose us. So, what gives us the right to disqualify ourselves?

We say God is perfect in all His ways, but when it comes to His selection of us, we deem Him unworthy of making the right decision. We must understand that every time we second guess God's selection, we second guess the same God we claim is all-knowing, all-powerful, and perfect.

In addition to being selected for the vision, God also selected us for the troubles that would come with the vision! God was confident that we were strong enough to endure the hell that would come with carrying out the vision because of what He placed on the inside of us. Before we ever made our entrance into the world, God knew what He desired us to do. He knew the answer He wanted us to bring to the earth. For that reason, He knitted us in our mother's wombs with everything we would need to be successful. As you ponder God's selection of you, just think about a boss preparing to select an employee for promotion. Doesn't he first consider the ability of the employee to handle the promotion? Of course, he does. The boss wants to protect his business and the investments he made in the business. He wouldn't promote someone into a position who could not carry the weight! In the same way, God carefully considered you for the vision and the mission. Now, it's up to you to accept and prepare!

As you move forward in your preparation, you must remind yourself that He chose you. God didn't make a mistake. He meant what He said, and He won't take it back. You have been selected! **Let's Pray!**

*Father God,*

*Thank you for trusting me. I know you are watching me day in and day out. You see my shortcomings, yet you still see fit to believe that I will make you proud. There have been times when I have doubted your capabilities because of my inability to be consistent. I am thankful that you do not operate like me. I am seeing more and more that you will continue to show yourself strong and mighty. You are the King of Glory (Psalm 24). Thank you for selecting me. In Jesus' Name, Amen.*

# WHAT ARE YOU
# WAITING FOR?

*"But there are some things that you cannot be sure of. You must take a chance. If you wait for perfect weather, you will never plant your seeds. If you are afraid that every cloud will bring rain, you will never harvest your crops." Ecclesiastes 11:4 (ERV)*

How many times have you used "waiting on God" as an excuse to sit still and do nothing? We've all done it before, but now is the time to kill that excuse. Waiting on God is not about sitting down, twiddling our fingers, and praying something will happen. Waiting on God requires us to prepare for what is on the way. Many of us believe that waiting on God requires us to wait for favorable conditions before we begin to take one step. This couldn't be further from the truth.

When we wait on God, we do what we can with what we already have. When we think we are waiting on God, God is actually waiting for us to make the next step. We selfishly want God to lay out the entire path before we move forward as if God is the one who is untrustworthy and inconsistent. God's track record is good. He's proven Himself to be faithful time and time again. On the other hand, we are not always so faithful to God and what He has purposed us to do.

This next season of your life is going to require complete obedience in the steps God has told you to take. You don't need all the start-up money to start planning the business. You don't need the five-bedroom house on the hill to start pursuing the marriage. You don't need the degree in hand to start preparing for your career. You only need to put your work where your faith is. Ask God what you can do to prepare for what He is about to do for you. Ask Him to reveal how you can start right where you are! Don't let waiting be your excuse. There is never a more perfect time to trust God outside of NOW! **Let's Pray!**

*Father God,*
   *I am thankful for my now and I am ready to prepare for my later. I know that the things you have prepared for me are waiting on me to come after them. Lord, rid my mind of making excuses. Help me not to operate out of fear, but to operate in my faith in you as my guide. I will be a good steward of the gift of time here on earth. I am grateful for every new day you give me. This life is short, however, it is the longest thing I will ever do. I will spend my days living for you. In Jesus' name, Amen.*

DAY THREE

# WRITE THE

# VISION

*"And the Lord answered me and said, Write the vision and engrave it so plainly upon tablets that everyone who passes may [be able to] read [it easily and quickly] as he hastens by."* Habakkuk 2:2 (AMP)

How many times have you laid awake at night dreaming about your goals? How many times have you daydreamed about all the things you've wanted to accomplish? Here's a better question: Why haven't your desires come to pass?

If you're like most people, you probably keep everything in your mind. When we keep our goals in our head, they tend to get clouded by everything else on our mind. For this reason, our goals remain dreams and never become our reality.

So, how do we take our goals from dreams to reality? We write them down! It doesn't matter how great you think your memory may be, a dull pencil beats a sharp mind any day! During this season of preparation, allow writing to become your friend. Just as God told Habakkuk to write the vision and make it plain, this is necessary for you as well. Writing your goals has many benefits. It allows you to measure your progress, kick procrastination, and also remember why you are doing whatever it is you are doing. As you write your vision and goals, it is important that you:

**Be Realistic**

Many of our goals never happen because we are unrealistic about what we desire to accomplish. Some things sound great, but are they realistic? For example, losing 50 pounds in a month sounds good, but is that goal realistic for you? As we write our goals, we must factor in everything required to see those goals happen. Don't base your goals upon what others have been able to do in a certain amount of time. We must make goals and timelines that work for our lives, responsibilities, and day to day schedules.

## Attach Your Why

As you write your goals, remember to write why they are important. Remembering why you are completing a thing will help you push through on those days you don't feel like working. Your why has the potential to wake you up early in the morning and keep you up at night. When we keep our why in the forefront of our goal planning, we can push through and become disciplined enough to see our goals completed.

## Put a Date on It

Someday soon, one day, in the near future, and sometime next year are not actual dates. Stop selling yourself dreams. Stamp each of your goals with a firm date of completion. Having a date on your goals will help you plan and prepare consistently.

## Keep It Visible

Don't write your goals and stick them in a notebook. Make a poster, jot it down on a sticky note, tape it to your wall, or whatever it takes for you to keep your vision in plain sight.

## Interact with Your Vision

Don't be afraid to adjust your goals as needed. If you don't make the first deadline, create a new deadline.

Whatever you do, don't change your desire to see the goal accomplished.

You deserve to see your goals come to life! With discipline, hard work, and faith, you will be on your way to accomplishing each goal God has placed on the inside of you. **Let's Pray!**

*Father God,*

*Thank you for the vision you have given me. The things I see in the natural do not compare to the revelations you are giving me in the spirit. As you reveal more and more to me concerning what is to come, increase in me the spirit of gratefulness. I never want to forget how far you've brought me while on this journey to getting where you have ordained me to be. Endow me with the spirit of tenacity so that as I execute your plan for me, I do not get off focus or side-tracked by the enemy. I know that you are still perfecting the things that concern me (Psalm 138:8), and for this, I say thank you. In Jesus' name, Amen.*

DAY FOUR

# SHUT UP!

*"Whoever guards his mouth preserves his life; he who opens wide his lips come to ruin."* Proverbs 13:3(ESV)

For whatever reason, we love to make sure people know that we are working hard and making things happen. The minute we create goals, our first notion is to announce it to anyone who will listen. Sometimes, we do it for support, but at other times, we do it for the validation.

Desiring validation is natural. As human beings, we naturally desire to know that what we are doing matters. If you've ever found yourself craving to be affirmed about your decisions, goals, and aspirations, don't feel bad. It is completely normal. A desire for affirmation becomes a bad thing when we seek the affirmation of people over the confirmation of God. Some people can only affirm what they have the guts to do. As a result, if your goals aren't realistic to them, they may shoot them down or cause you to feel as though they are unattainable. What God has shown you is not for everyone's consumption. God showed YOU because He knew YOU had the faith level to see it through. When it's a God-thing, you don't need the validation of anyone else. Be careful not to expose yourself to the opinions of others. Stop making announcements and just make moves. The support of people is welcomed, but it is not always needed.

Can we be honest for a moment? Everyone is not rooting for our success. In the Bible, Elisha told his servant not to fear, because there were more for them than against them. We typically read this and shout over the fact that there are more for us, but overlook the warning that there are some who are against us. Being aware that there are some who are not in our corner allows us to protect ourselves from negative backlash about what God has called us to do. When we are unaware, the voice of those against us can sometimes become louder than the voices cheering us to the finish line. In this season of preparation, you can't afford to give everyone front row seats to your race. God has spoken in peace to you concerning the next area of your life. You must protect that peace, even if it means keeping everything to yourself until it is complete.

If God said it, just allow it to be so.  God is going to be God in your life. Rest in His provision, and not the pleasure of people. Now is not the time for you to have diarrhea at the mouth. It is not necessary to tell everyone, everything. Guard your mouth and stop telling everyone where God is about to take you. You don't have to announce your elevation. God is about to place you on a public platform for all to see. You will be ready for it because of the preparation you performed in silence and the work that took place in private. Put a "shhhhhush" on it and shut your mouth! **Let's Pray!**

*Father God,*

*As excited as I am about all the amazing things that are to come, I understand that I must not allow my excitement to get the best of me. It is your will that I prosper in every area of my life. Every move you make on my behalf privately does not need to be broadcasted publically. Lord, help me to keep a humble heart and a grateful praise in my spirit so I do not taint the excellence of your purpose as I await your release and elevation of me. In Jesus' Name, Amen.*

DAY FIVE

## SEEK

# THE SOURCE

*"As they approached the Temple, a man lame from birth was being carried in. Each day he was put beside the Temple gate, the one called the Beautiful Gate, so he could beg from the people going into the Temple."*
Acts 3:2 (NLT)

God created us to be connected to each other. He designed mankind to support, uplift, love, and care for one another. While it has always been His desire for us to be there for one another, He did not create us to be each other's source. Many of us make the mistake of making our jobs, relationships, and friendships the source of our provision, protection, and encouragement. When those things fall short, as they always will, we are then left feeling empty, alone, and discouraged.

As we prepare, we must remember that God is our only true source. Everything flows from Him, so all we are and all we hope to become is in who He is. God chooses to use people based on their obedience. If no one gets in line to do what God has told them to do for you, rest assured that God is still going to show Himself mighty and strong in your life. Everything we have comes from God, though it may come through people. Although we go to doctors to be healed, the healing we receive comes from God. We can work for a check, but the provision still comes from God. We can seek others for encouragement and advice, but the wisdom still comes from God. Once we allow ourselves to put everything in this perspective, we will stop having expectations of the resource, and place our trust in the Source.

Depending on resources will eventually leave us empty. Even the resource needs the replenishment of God! If God doesn't replenish it, it becomes empty. As you prepare, remember that God is your true and ultimate source. Seek Him for what you need, and thank Him for the way He chooses to provide it. Never allow yourself to become so enamored with God's route of provision that you overlook His power of provision. **Let's Pray!**

*Father God,*

*Forgive me. All this time I have been asking people to give me the things you have already blessed me with. I have been looking to people to love me in a way that only you can. Lord, you have never slacked in your promises concerning me, and for this, I say thank you! As of today, I am commanding my focus to shift back to you, where it should have always been. I thank you for all the resources you have granted me in people and in things, however, I thank you even the more for being THE source from which the resources come. God, you are amazing and I honor you for being who you are in my life and in this world. In Jesus' name, Amen.*

DAY SIX

# FAITH IT

# OUT

*"For we walk by faith, not by sight."* 2 Corinthians 5:7 (ESV)

When we first make the decision to follow whatever vision God has placed in our hearts, we sometimes make the mistake of believing that the hard part is over. I regret to inform you that this is only the beginning. After we make the decision to carry out what God has assigned us to do, our next step must be to walk.

The minute we begin to walk, we get hit with doubt, worry, fear, and concerns. We find ourselves contemplating if we made the right decision, if we actually heard God, if the timing is right, the list goes on. Despite what we may feel, we must remind ourselves to keep walking.

The scripture for today tells us that we must walk by faith, and not by sight. Understand that walking by faith does not omit us from trouble. Trouble comes from the enemy to stop us from walking, but God allows us to experience trouble so that our faith is perfected.

No matter what we are dealing with or what life throws at us, we must be willing to walk. As we walk, we must constantly decide if we are going to trust our faith or our sight. Trusting our sight limits our walk. When we take steps depending upon what we see, we can easily find ourselves in a place where we aren't moving at all. When we catch a glimpse of trouble, our natural instincts are to freeze or flee. Just think about the last time you saw trouble coming your way. You either froze in place or ran in the opposite direction. The same thing happens to us as it relates to our goals and visions.

Our natural sight is conditioned to see obstacles, whereas our faith sees the way through the obstacle. Our sight helps us to see the problem ahead, but our faith allows us to see God's promised provision. When we trust our sight, our walk is limited. When we trust faith, our walk becomes unlimited.

If we are ever to experience the joy God has set before us, we must continue to walk by faith, and not what our situations appear to be. Our eyes will lie to us, but faith in God will never steer us wrong. In this season, what will you allow to lead you to your destination? **Let's Pray!**

*Father God,*

*Thank you for being in control of every aspect of my life. Thank you for stretching me in order to perfect me for your purpose and glory. Lord, I ask that as you test my faithfulness, you increase my capacity to withstand the tough times that are sure to come. As I have faith in you, I ask you to have faith in me that I will remain consistent in you. In you God, there is no failure and so I claim victory over every test and trial that comes my way. When it is all said and done, you will receive all the honor and praise. In Jesus' name, Amen.*

DAY SEVEN

# CAN YOU

# HEAR?

*"He let you hear his voice from heaven so he could instruct you. He let you see his great fire here on earth so he could speak to you from it."*
*Deuteronomy 4:36 (NLT)*

One of the most frustrating things we experience in preparation is feeling like we can't hear God. At some point in our journey, we all have felt as though God is no longer speaking to us. An inability to hear God comes from three things.

**We haven't done what He has already instructed us to do.**

When you were a child, I'm sure you experienced your parents becoming frustrated with telling you to do the same thing over and over again. Eventually, it came to a point where they looked at you and said absolutely nothing. You knew what that look meant, and you also knew that their silence hinted that correction was on the way. In our relationship with God, we sometimes disobey what He has told us to do because of fear, disobedience, or a lack of faith. The thing is, He won't release the next thing until you take care of the now thing. If you feel as though you can't hear God, the first thing you should do is check your obedience to the last thing He instructed you to do.

**We are listening to our distractions.**

How can we expect to hear God in the middle of all the distractions we've given our ear to? Sometimes, the reason we can't hear God is because we are so busy listening to everything and everyone else. God is a jealous God, but He will not compete with what you have freely chosen to listen to. When you are ready to shut the door to your distractions and attune your ear to the voice of God, He will speak to you and provide encouragement and instruction for this season of your life.

**We only expect to hear God in one way.**

Because God is so multi-dimensional, we cannot limit the way He desires to speak to us. God speaks to us in many different ways. He will send wise people, teachers, preachers, or prophets to share His word with us. Sometimes, He speaks to us through situations, circumstances, and other life matters. His favorite way of speaking to us is through His Word. We can read the same scripture and get various revelations at different times of our lives. Don't condition your ears to hear God in one specific way. Be open to hearing God, however, He desires to speak to you.

If you ever find yourself in a place where you can't hear God clearly, review these three points and make the necessary adjustments. You can't afford not to hear from God in your season of preparation. His voice, instruction, and encouragement are vital to your success. **Let's Pray!**

*Father God,*

*As I take the necessary steps these to prepare to receive my hearts desires, help me to keep my heart and mind set on you! Before I seek you for anything, I want to thank you for everything. As I pray this prayer, you are already increasing my faith in you. I trust that you are going to do exactly what you said you would do. I believe that in faith, by making my requests known unto you, you will give me the strength and the courage to walk forward in your name. You have called me to operate in excellence and I am starting by having full confidence in you. I know that if I stay connected to The Source, I will never be without a resource and for this I give you all the glory, honor, and praise. In Jesus' name, Amen!*

# FEAR IS NOT A FACTOR
# FOR YOU

*"For God has not given us a spirit of fear and timidity, but of power, love, and self-discipline."* 2 Timothy 1:7 (NLT)

God has not given us a spirit of fear. It is not okay to have fear in our hearts or minds. Many of us have allowed fear to become a part of who we are. We fail to realize that fear has the capability to choke the life out of anything we put our hands to work.

Fear can set in from circumstances, failure, rejection, abandonment, etc. Sometimes, we endure tough situations, and instead of pulling out the lesson, we pull out the fear to never try again. In our preparation for what we do not see, we must be careful not to prepare from a place of fear.

Fear causes us to limit ourselves, our goals, capabilities, and God's movement in our lives. Fear places a ceiling on everything we desire to do. Fear lies and tells us that we can only go so high before we fall. Fear says that even if we tried, we would still fail. Fear is dangerous to any believer because it is in direct opposition to faith.

When we prepare from a place of fear, we place safety nets around ourselves. These safety nets can come in the form of a Plan B or a back-up plan to God's Ultimate plan. Here's the issue with that. If we create a back-up plan for God's plan, what we are ultimately saying is that God won't hold true to His promises. This says that God, in all of His infinite wisdom, needs your finite strategy and planning. This says that God, the one we lean and depend on, needs to depend on YOU.

I'm sure it didn't take much thought for you to understand how jacked up this perspective is. God doesn't need you to create a back-up for His plan. His word is His word. It shall not return to Him void. As you prepare, be sure to check your place of preparation. Will we always get it right? No. However, it is not our place to develop a plan for if we mess up. All of our energy should be directed to successfully achieving what God has set before us. If we fall along the way, it is God's job to catch us. There are many ways to determine if you are preparing from a place of fear. Let's review two of them.

**You are planning based on what you have.**

We should always start where we are, not finish where we are. If our goals and visions can be completed based on what we are able to provide right now, there is no need for God's provision. God's plan for our lives always supersedes what we could ask or think. So, if you are preparing based on what YOU can do, it's not completely God's vision. Your goals should make you nervous. Nervousness is a sign that you are aware that what you are doing requires you to trust God. Fear on the other hand, cause you to scale back and stick to what you know you can do.

**Your plans will only benefit you.**

Sometimes, we only try to benefit ourselves because we are afraid to fail others. We are okay if we let ourselves down, but to involve others and potentially let them down is too much for our minds to fathom. For that reason, we create goals and dreams that will only benefit us, even when God has told us that it will benefit others. If your goals and visions will only benefit you, you may need to check your heart for fear.

The bottom line is this: God has not given you a spirit of fear. He has given each of us power, love, and a sound mind. In this season of preparation, daily cancel out fear and choose to walk boldly in the authority God has given you. **Let's Pray!**

*Father God,*

*I can be honest and say that living a life of faith has not been easy. The more I seek your face and focus on you, the easier it gets. Lord, I know your word tells me not to worry because it is you who will bring the harvest according to the seeds I have planted. Lord, you have provided the tools I need to successfully till the ground. I will continue to plow and plant until YOU say otherwise. I am not afraid of my tomorrow because just as you hold me in the palm of your hand, you hold tomorrow as well. Thank you, God, for reminding me to plan for my tomorrow, today. In Jesus' name, Amen*

.

# FIX YOUR
# FACE

*"For as he thinks in his heart, so is he. "Eat and drink!" he says to you, But his heart is not with you."*
Proverbs 23:7 (NKJV)

We've all heard the saying, "Your attitude determines your altitude." How often do we take the time to consider how much of an impact our attitude can have on our elevation? In our preparation, we cannot overlook the adjustments that must be made in our attitude.

I've encountered so many individuals who flaunt their nasty attitudes and expect people to accept it because "That's just who they are." The sad thing about this is, we have family and friends who deal with it, so we naturally expect the rest of the world to put up with it. When people refuse to "adjust" to our attitudes, we quickly write them off. If a boss can't get "with the program," we leave the job and find somewhere else to work. If the church doesn't cater to it, we run off with self-created church hurt and find a church that will.

In all of our running, we have to eventually realize that the problem is not everyone else. The problem is us. People like this eventually find themselves alone and stagnant. Here's the thing: People don't have to deal with your attitude. As a leader, I can honestly tell you that I would rather work with someone who is not as talented, but has good character, than deal with a talented individual who does not know how to treat others.

Before we go higher, we must ensure that our attitude can keep us there. How bad would it be for people to want our gift, but want us to stay at home?

Rolling your eyes, snapping your fingers, and popping your lips aren't the only way you can have a bad attitude. Being ungrateful, hateful, and rude are also indicators that your attitude is not in check. Some of us even have closed off attitudes, where we are not inviting to people. Negative attitudes operate as a repellent to destiny. If we expect to fulfill our destiny, we must check our attitudes.

We all have bad days. There will be days where we don't want to deal with people. There will be moments where our circumstances make us want to do everything but smile. As leaders in the body of Christ, we cannot allow our negative attitudes to have a lasting impact on what we are called to do. We have to deal with the issues of our hearts in private so that we don't harm others or delay our destiny. As you make the necessary adjustments to your attitude, ask God to search your heart and expose areas to you that you need to work on. Everything flows from our hearts. The first step to adjusting our attitudes is to check what is harboring in our hearts. **Let's Pray!**

*Father God,*

*Before I allow my attitude to become infected by my current circumstances, give me a double portion of your spiritual fruit. Father, to be effective in this walk of faith in you, I need more of your love, joy, peace, patience, kindness, goodness, faithfulness, gentleness, and self-control (Galatians 5:22-23). I never want to be a negative representation of you, because you have called me to be a light in this dark world. Lord, there are people here on the Earth that you have assigned me to, but before I am able to reach them, I must reach you. I ask that you erase the residue of what is and what has been concerning my negative emotions and give me a new positive perspective on life and the calling you have placed over me. In Jesus' name, Amen.*

# THE SPIRIT OF

# OFFENSE

*"Don't pay attention to everything people say—you may hear your servant insulting you, and you know yourself that you have insulted other people many times."* Ecclesiastes 7:21-22 (GNT)

I n a "perfect world" everyone would think the same, speak alike, and view life from the same perspective. We would all march to the same beat, no one would ever disagree, and everyone would always be on the same page. Unfortunately, this is not the case. As a matter of fact, God intentionally created us to be different. We all see things differently, create different solutions, and bring different ideas to the table. If we learned to embrace our differences, we could get a lot done in less time. One of the biggest issues that hinder us from using our differences for good is the spirit of offense.

No successful person has ever done anything worthy of being remembered on their own. As you are elevated, you will find yourself dealing with more and more people from different walks of life. You cannot afford for Kingdom work to be halted because you are easily offended. Don't get me wrong, offense happens. Sometimes, people are intentionally offensive, but at other times, they aren't. You can't control others, however, you can control how you ingest what they say, and also, how you respond to it. Here are five principles that will help you deal with offense.

**Talk yourself off the ledge.**

Offense doesn't just happen. We either go into situations expecting it or think about it non-stop the moment it happens.  Just as you think yourself into being offended, you can think yourself out of it.

**Put yourself in the offender's shoes.**

I challenge you to think about the time someone accused you of offending them. Nine times out of ten, you didn't mean it, and you didn't see how in the world what you said or did could have offended them. In your moments of offense, put yourself in your offender's shoes. Often, we judge ourselves based on our intentions, but we judge others based upon their actions. Before you react, take some time and think if they intended to offend you. After some thought, you will probably realize that they did not mean it the way you perceived it.

**Learn humility.**

Most offense happens when our pride has been hit. We present a new idea or concept, someone doesn't agree with it, and boom, we're offended. Pride convinces us that our way is the best way. When we learn to humble ourselves, we can listen to the opinions of others without feeling attacked.

**Seek truth over self-righteousness.**

Some of us will do anything just to be right, even at the cost of covering the truth. One of the most important keys to not being offended is always to seek the truth. Sometimes, the truth may cause our ideas to be thrown out, but that's okay. Our desire should always be the truth, rather than the comfort of a lie.

**Overcome self-centeredness.**

Being self-centered causes us always to take on the victim mentality. Every situation is always about how someone offended us, but never how we may have offended them. When we allow ourselves to break free of self-centeredness, we learn that others have feelings too. Most of the time, the same respect and listening ear we desire, they desire as well.

Before your next team planning meeting, take some time and meditate about your issue with offense. If you need to jot these points on a sticky note, do that. Whatever you do, don't allow the spirit of offense to hinder you from where God desires to take you! **Let's Pray!**

*Father God,*

*Before I search outward, show me who I am inward. There have been times when I have operated out of my flesh and have offended someone knowingly as well as unknowingly. Right now, I take a moment to plead for forgiveness. Teach me the right way to handle conflict so that when it comes, I can deal with it in a way that will allow peace to come into the situation. Lord, show me how to get outside of myself so that I never get so 'big' that I forget how I felt when I was 'small'. I need your spirit to rest on my emotions so I can take on the victor mentality instead of the*

56

victim mindset. Let your Holy Spirit bring back to my remembrance the words I will need to encourage myself in you at any given time. In Jesus' name, Amen.

DAY ELEVEN

## JUST KEEP
# SWIMMING

*"The LORD directs the steps of the godly. He delights in every detail of their lives. Though they stumble, they will never fall, for the LORD holds them by the hand." Psalms 37:23-24 (NLT)*

Disappointments and failures have a way of knocking the very breath from our bodies. When things don't turn out the way we planned, we often feel defeated and are discouraged to try again. After trying so hard and putting your best foot forward, it's hard to believe that your efforts were all for nothing. No matter how successful we become, we all face moments of discouragement. Don't believe me, just research your favorite celebrity, leader, or person of influence. I'm positive you will be able to find at least one story of a disappointing moment in their lives.

One character trait anyone who desires to be successful must acquire is a quick recovery time. Many of us are not yet where we desire to be because of the last failure or setback. Taking time to breath is necessary, but we must not stay in the place of defeat. After we have caught our breath and assessed what went wrong/what we could do better, we must keep swimming. Setbacks can knock you down, but they can't keep you down! When you set a goal to achieve something, you've got to stay committed until you see your desired results.

Do you think Steve Jobs got it right the first time? What about the second, third, or fourth time? I'll bet it took a few tries for him to get it right. What if he gave up the first time he got it wrong? We wouldn't have the amazing products we have grown to love today.

Now, I want you to think about you and what you are working on. Has disappointment crippled your ability to work? You have no idea how the world needs the very thing you are working on. If you give up now, you'll never know or understand the value of what you are producing.

I know it can be hard to bounce back after a hard hit, but you've got to remind yourself to just keeping swimming! This is not the end. This is only the beginning of better! **Let's Pray!**

*Father God,*

*I thank you right now for guiding my steps. Lord, you never promised me that my walk with you would be easy, so I know that the stronger my relationship with you grows, the harder this life here on earth may become, and God, I am okay with that. Jesus, I know that if you care so much for the animals of this earth then as your child, your loving care has no limits for me. Thank you for being my Father. I accept the call you have on my life and come hell or high water, I will "just keep swimming" and carry on in your name! In Jesus' name, Amen.*

DAY TWELVE

# EXPECTANCY

*"I wait for the LORD, my whole being waits, and in his word I put my hope."* Psalm 130:5 *(NIV)*

I've gone to quite a few track and field events. One of my favorite races to watch is the relay race. The most amazing thing about the relay race is that everyone on the relay team has a specific role to play in order for their team to win the race. From the outside, it appears that each person is just sitting waiting for the baton to be passed to them, but there is much more to it. Not only do the runners wait, but they wait in expectancy. Today, we are going to discuss the difference waiting in expectancy makes in our season of preparation.

The word expectation is defined as the strong belief that something will happen. When we are in expectancy that something will happen, we plan for it, and we prepare for it. Let's go back to the runners in the relay race. As the runners wait for the baton to be passed to them, they watch their surroundings. They watch the runners in front of them. They watch the baton as it makes its way around to them. The runner waits in expectancy because he knows that even though the baton may have to go around the track, sooner rather than later, the baton is going to find its way in his hand! When it does, he can't waste a second getting ready to run. He has to be ready to run the minute the baton touches his hand!

What if a runner waits until the baton gets into his hand to prepare to run? His lack of preparation could potentially cost his team the entire race. What does this say to us? As we wait with hope that God will come through, we must wait in expectation. We must prepare for the very thing we are waiting for God to do.

The concept of waiting in expectancy is not difficult when it comes to some things. For instance, when we expect money to come, what do we do? We begin to make plans for it before it even hits our accounts. When parents are expecting a child, they begin to prepare for the baby by purchasing the things a baby needs. However, when we have to wait for the things we don't have physical proof of, we sometimes experience difficulty. In this season of preparation, I encourage you not to complain, but to prepare. How sad would it be for it to be your turn, but you are not ready to take off? **Let's Pray!**

*Father God,*
*You have told me not to be anxious for anything. My human nature wants everything quick, fast, and easy. My spirit man urges me to trust your timing in all things. Lord, as I pray, teach me to be quiet so that I can fully hear your response to me. As I wait on you, I will wait in good cheer because I believe the blessings you have for me are too amazing not to joyfully wait on! Thank you, God, for increasing my faith as I continue to wait in expectancy! In Jesus' name, Amen.*

# CAN YOU BE
# TRUSTED?

*"Then the LORD said to Satan, "Have you noticed my servant Job? No one else on earth is like him. He is an honest and innocent man, honoring God and staying away from evil." Job 1:8 (NCV)*

With our seasons constantly changing, life can sometimes feel like one big rat race. As you prepare for what you do not see, it is important to understand that there is a reason for everything we endure.

Most of what we go through is to build our endurance and strength for the next season. God wants to know that we will be more faithful to Him than we are to our emotions and environments. In our scripture focus for today, God suggested Job because he knew that Job could be trusted. As we prepare, we need to pose the question to ourselves, "Can God trust me with trials, trouble, and triumph?" Each of these three tests reveals something different about how we respond to life.

**Trials**

Trials are significant events of our lives in which our faith, love, and trust in God are tested. A trial can be the loss of a loved one, getting fired from a job, failing a major academic test, or a bad break-up. In these moments, God is testing us on the lessons we've learned leading up to that moment. Have you ever been studying a particular thing in scripture, and days later you are tested in that area? For instance, you've been studying patience, then suddenly you are put in a situation where your patience is tested? This is a trial. During trials, it is important that you remember what you've learned in that season. How you pass the test of trials determine whether or not you are ready for the next season. If you fail, you must go back and learn before you can move forward. Trials can seem unfair and taxing, but think about this: Why would God advance you to the next level if He knows that you have not retained the information of this level? Remember that God's plan is for us to prosper. If it seems as though you are constantly being faced with the same trial, you need to figure out what lesson you've been overlooking and allow grace to teach you how to do better the next time around.

## Troubles

Unlike trials, troubles are situations that constantly nag and irritate us. Troubles can be compared to the thorn Paul describes in 2 Corinthians. You may experience trouble in maintaining your finances, dealing with crazy family, or working on difficult tasks. During our troubles, our consistency in responding God's way is being tested. God wants to know that we won't get weary or be caught off guard. Unlike trials, troubles come our way daily, and we must always choose to respond the right way. Our daily response to trouble builds our endurance.

## Triumph

Yes, there are tests in triumph. God observes us in triumph because He desires to know how well we can stand after a victory. If we aren't careful, our current victory can be the killer of our next victory. During triumph, we must remember to build monuments and keep moving to the next thing God desires us to accomplish. Many of us make the mistake of becoming so drunk with celebration that we do not properly prepare for the next big thing.

In your preparation, you are sure to experience trials, trouble, and triumph. You can't afford to be caught off guard, so please heed this warning. Your response in every situation determines whether or not you can be trusted with the next level. **Let's Pray!**

*Father God,*

*While I do strive to be all that you have created me to be, I know that anything I do cannot be done without you (2 Corinthians 3:4-6). As much as I do not want trouble to come my way, I understand that trouble comes to test me and make me stronger. Lord, I want to be an example of how your glory manifests in the Earth. Just as I trust you to continue to be you in all your splendor, you can trust that I will always obey and depend on you whether in trial, trouble, or triumph. God, you can consider me! From this day forward, I will no longer question your plan when trouble comes. I will push through in your name. When the victory is won, I will be able to tell the world how you brought me through. God, you will get all the glory from my story. In Jesus' name, Amen.*

DAY FOURTEEN

# ACCOUNTABILITY

*"Confess your sins to each other and pray for each other so that you may be healed. The earnest prayer of a righteous person has great power and produces wonderful results."* James 5:16 (NLT)

I f you take a look at the circles of successful individuals, you will notice one thing that is consistent across the board: They all have a level of accountability. Rather it is in the form of an accountant, manager, spiritual advisor, etc., all successful individuals have a level of accountability. Many people overlook the need for accountability, and as a result, they find themselves in stressful situations and circumstances that they brought upon themselves through carelessness. Instead of looking at accountability as being bossed around by another individual, we must begin to view accountability as a protection of God's investment.

Who fills a house with nice things and fails to install some type of alarm system? Only someone who doesn't care much about what they've invested in. If you want to see how much individual values their investments, take a look at how they protect them. Accountability is God's way of protecting everything He has placed on the inside of us. It holds us to our commitment to the progression that must take place in our lives. When He places people in our lives to hold us accountable, it is not His desire for those individuals to replace Him. He desires those individuals to protect the gifting, talent, and purpose He's given to you by acting as parameters around the decisions you make and the actions you take. When done God's way, accountability develops a sense of responsibility, promotes integrity, and prevents us from doing something just because we can do it. Additionally, accountability promotes a healthy self-examination, protects you from unwise relationships, and promotes a Godly attitude and spirit. There are so many benefits to accountability. The season you are preparing for requires you to have a circle of accountability. Over the next few days, we will discuss two types of accountability- accountability partners, and mentors. As we discuss, be sure to be prayerful about the accountability you will install for the next season of your life. **Let's Pray!**

*Father God,*

*In Proverbs, you tell us that iron sharpens iron, so one person sharpens another. Thank you for assigning people to my circle to keep me sharp. Thank you for placing a vault of protection around me in the form of accountability. Give me the wisdom to utilize those in my circle who have the grace to handle the mantel on my life. Even if you must alter my circle, I yield to your leadership, and I trust you to plant the people I need in my life for this season and seasons to come. In Jesus' Name, Amen.*

DAY FIFTEEN

# IDENTIFYING AN ACCOUNTABILITY PARTNER

*"As iron sharpens iron, so a friend sharpens a friend."*
Proverbs 27:17 (NLT)

Welcome to Day 15. We will continue our discussion on accountability from Day 14. Today, we will discuss accountability partners. Accountability partners are individuals who are as goal-driven as you are. The two of you should be on or around the same level spiritually. Having an accountability partner is a two-way street, so you must be strategic in your selection of an accountability partner. As you observe those around you, keep in mind these nine points of accountability.

## A Relationship with God

Your accountability partner must have a relationship with God. They must also have a consistent prayer life. As stated before, they should be on the same spiritual level as you. If you can't miss a Sunday at church, don't choose an accountability partner who barely wakes up in time for service. Your focus has to be the same, and you must be aiming towards similar levels of operation. You don't have to be in the same career or field, but a relationship with God is a must for your accountability partner.

## Trustworthy

Asking someone to be your accountability partner requires openness and honesty on an entirely different level. You want to ensure that your accountability partner is someone who won't air your dirty laundry the second they get a chance. A good way to observe if an individual is trustworthy is by listening to the things they say about those they are close to. If they are known to gossip, nine times out of ten, they won't make a trustworthy accountability partner.

**Provides Spiritual Wisdom Rather Than Opinion**

Here's the thing: Everyone has an opinion. As the saying goes, we are all entitled to an opinion. Your accountability partner should be one who will give you spiritual wisdom when you need it. They should be spiritually mature enough to provide advice based on God's word, not what they feel.

**Courage to Confront You, Strength to Cover You**

Sometimes, those closest to us are uncomfortable with telling us when we are wrong, if our idea doesn't make sense, or if something we are doing isn't smart. Your accountability partner must be courageous enough to tell you these things. They can't be a yes-man. In addition to being courageous enough to check you, they must also have the strength to cover you in prayer. Even when you make unwise decisions, your accountability partner should be able to cover you in prayer and stick to what they hear, no matter how you may feel about it.

**Vision for Your Now and Later**

Your accountability partner should be able to see where you are now, and where you are headed. This is important because their expectations of you should align with your future. Your accountability partner should be able to check you for growth. It would be impossible for them to do this if they have no foresight about the person you are to become.

## Capability to Forgive

The truth of the matter is, you will make mistakes. You won't always get everything right. Your accountability partner should be an individual who knows how to forgive quickly. They must also have a quick recovery time. If you are going to partner in accountability with anyone, you don't have time to be holding grudges and dealing with offense. The lines of communication must remain open and honest at all times.

## Encourager, not an Enabler

There is a difference between encouraging someone and enabling them. Your accountability partner should encourage you to be the best you can be, but they should not enable you to do things that are not wise.

## A Good Listener

A good listener knows when someone needs to vent, when someone needs advice, and when someone needs prayer. Your accountability partner should be able to listen and know the difference. A good listener also knows how to ask questions for clarity and understanding.

## Always Has Your Best Interests at Heart

At the end of the day, your accountability partner should always have your best interests in mind. They cannot be secretly jealous of your success. They must be secure in who they are and possess the ability to be genuinely happy for you. Also, be sure that your accountability partner doesn't secretly wish they were in your shoes. Again, they must be sure in who they are and what they are called to do in order to hold you accountable for anything.

As you begin to search for an accountability partner, be sure to keep these points of accountability in mind. Remember, you need accountability for where you are headed. Be prayerful in your selection. **Let's Pray!**

*Father God,*

*Thank you for your guidance thus far. I thank you for leaving me the ultimate accountability partner, your Holy Spirit (John 14:16,18). The Holy Spirit is with me to comfort and keep me as I grow through life. God, right now I ask that you will reveal to me who I need to have in my life as an accountability partner. Send to me not only a friend, but someone who has the propensity to check me and cover me at the same time from a place of love and understanding. As much as I would like to think that I can 'fix' me without outside influences, I know you did not design me to walk this walk alone. God, I thank you for sending me a person to remind me of the task at hand. In Jesus' name, Amen.*

# THE MAKINGS OF A GOOD
# MENTOR

*"Give instruction to a wise man, and he will be still wiser; teach a righteous man, and he will increase in learning." Proverbs 9:9 (ESV)*

A mentor is a different form of accountability. Whereas having an accountability partner is a two-way street, a mentor is a one-way street. A mentor is in your life for the main purpose of pouring into you and holding you accountable to becoming your very best. Let's chat briefly about the makings of a good mentor.

**Fruit**

You should be able to see the fruit of the good decisions they've made over the course of their life. A mentor doesn't have to be in the same lane as you are. Drive, determination, and fight are consistent across the board. Your mentor should be able to provide constructive criticism. You can't take constructive criticism from someone who has never constructed anything. As you search for a mentor, be sure to check their fruit! While you should not idolize or covet anything they have, you should be able to view their lives and see what they have produced.

**This is not a friendship.**

Although you and your mentor may build a lifelong connection, make no mistake, your mentor is not in your life to be your friend. They shouldn't call you with their problems, or spend most of your time together complaining about the things that are going on in their lives. Remember, mentoring is a one-way street. The purpose of them being your mentor is to pour into you, not the other way around.

**Transparency**

Your mentor must be willing to be transparent about how they got where they are now. They should feel comfortable with sharing strategy and ideas to help you do what you are doing better. A good mentor will never withhold the pour. Their desire should be to give you everything they have to offer.

**Honesty**

No one knows everything, so don't expect your mentor to have all the answers. You should, however, expect them to be honest. A good mentor will let you know that they don't have all the answers but will work with you to find them.

**Challenging**

Your mentor should challenge you. You should be comfortable enough to express where you fall short but uncomfortable enough to seek change. A mentor should challenge the way you think and how you operate.

I don't care how much you've been able to acquire on your own, this next season of your life demands that you have accountability in place. **Let's Pray!**

*Father God,*

*As I search for a mentor, I pray that you would lead me in the path of the individual who would be the best fit for what you have planned for my life. You are Alpha and Omega. You know my beginning, and you know my end. From where I stand in my life, I can only see my right now. Help me to pinpoint the individual who will not only serve my right now, but also my future. In Jesus' name, Amen.*

DAY SEVENTEEN

# STRETCH

*"Then He said to the man, 'Stretch out your hand.'
And he stretched it out, and it was restored whole
like the other."*
Matthew 12:13 (MEV)

In our scripture focus today, Jesus tells the man with the withered hand to stretch forth his hand. Reading this scripture, one may get confused as to why Jesus instructed him to stretch his hand, instead of pulling his hand out for him. Here's why, whenever God gives us the command, he also gives us the ability. Jesus was able to instruct the man to stretch out his hand because he had already given him the ability to do so.

There is no greater display of faith than preparing for what you do not see. This requires us to stretch beyond what we know and where we are comfortable. In this season of preparation, I'm sure you've realized by now that you cannot stay in the same place you've always been. Your next will require you to stretch beyond what you've always known and how you've always operated. It even requires us to stretch beyond what we already have. The greatest concern of any visionary or leader is that they will not have the financial support or people support they need to carry out what God has placed on the inside of them. Here's the thing: When God gave you the vision, he never consulted your bank account or your circles of influence. He didn't call a meeting with your insecurities, your past, or your fears. Whenever God gives us anything, He ensures that we have everything we need to get it done.

Will it be uncomfortable? Yes. Will it feel strange? Yes. Will you sometimes feel alone? Yes. Keep in mind that nothing great has ever been birthed in a place of comfort. If you are uncomfortable and feel stretched, you are in the perfect position to release what God has placed on the inside of you! **Let's Pray!**

*Father God,*

*You have begun a great work in my life! I can see your glory manifesting with every new day. I praise you for restoring the damaged areas of my heart. I thank you for the ability to be stretched yet not tear. I worship you because you are so great to me when I can only be good to you. Lord, as I take my level of preparation to another level, grant me the wisdom to employ divine strategy towards the task at hand. As much as I desire for you to do new things in my life, my desire first, is that you be larger than life, IN my life. I thank you, Father that this is only the beginning! In Jesus' name, Amen.*

# REST IN HELL, PROCRASTINATION

*"Take your son, your only son—yes, Isaac, whom you love so much—and go to the land of Moriah. Go and sacrifice him as a burnt offering on one of the mountains, which I will show you. ³ The next morning Abraham got up early. He saddled his donkey and took two of his servants with him, along with his son, Isaac. Then he chopped wood for a fire for a burnt offering and set out for the place God had told him about."* Genesis 22:2-3 (NLT)

You can walk into any room of leaders or visionaries, whisper the word procrastination, and watch as every person in the room begins to roll their eyes. Procrastination is one of the most common hindrances for many of us. Before we deal with how to kick procrastination, let's discuss why we procrastinate in the first place.

When God tells us to do something, our minds instantly go to all that it would take to get it done. Instead of focusing on the first step we were commanded to take, we begin to overwhelm ourselves with the details of what is to come. For this reason, many of us never take the first step, no matter how simple it may be. On the other hand, some of us are just plain lazy. We want better, and we desire to be used by God, however, we aren't willing to do the work required to see all our dreams become a reality. Here's the thing. Often, when we think about procrastination, we think about how it affects us. Have you ever taken a moment and thought about how your procrastination may affect someone else? Someone out there is waiting on what God has called us to do. Every second we spend in disobedience is another second that those individuals go without what they need to be successful. The next time you think about procrastinating on what God has told you to do, think about the many individuals you are impacting as well.

Biblically, whenever a miracle took place, it occurred because of someone's immediate response to the word of God. What miracles could you be holding up because you refuse to act on what God has told you to do? As we prepare for what we cannot see, we have to give procrastination the benediction. In this next season of our lives, we can't afford to procrastinate on what God has told us to do.

Whenever God commands you to do a thing, act on it immediately. Don't concern yourself with the next steps that will follow. When God told Abraham to move, Abraham did as God instructed him. The details came as he continued to walk. Don't worry about what will come next. Trust God and know that if He told you to go, He has a plan that He will reveal as you begin to walk. You can't get the next set of instructions if you aren't obedient to the steps you already have. Here are a few great ways to beat procrastination.

**Get a planner and actually use it.**

Interact with your planner daily. Keep it close to you and make a habit of writing down the things you have to do and when you need to have them completed. Check off items as you complete them to give yourself a sense of accomplishment.

**Create distraction free moments.**

Sometimes, it feels like whenever we get ready to do anything constructive, we are confronted with thousands of distractions. At the beginning of every day, practice turning off every distraction and focus on tackling everything on your to-do list. Try this for 30 minutes to an hour every day.

**Just do it.**

One of the best ways to beat laziness and procrastination is just to start doing it. As you begin to work, you will gain the energy, and the desire to keep going.

The truth of the matter is, we won't always feel like doing what needs to be done. We can beat those moments by creating smart habits of productivity. Procrastination may have worked on other levels of your life, but I assure you, procrastination will not be your friend where God desires to take you next! **Let's Pray!**

*Father God,*

*As much as I want things to happen when I want them to, I honor and respect the fact that your timing is always best. You know the ins and outs of my life, and when I submit my plans to your purpose, everything falls into place. Lord, I ask that you help me to extinguish the spirit of procrastination that has made its way into multiple areas of my life. While waiting until the last minute has worked before, I understand that my old ways will not open new doors. God, help me to wait when you say wait and to launch out when you say launch out. I always want to be in position. My desire is to be willing and ready to do what it is you have called me to do. No longer will I delay your work. God, continue to stretch me and mold me into the best version of me. In Jesus' name, Amen.*

DAY NINETEEN

## PACE

# YOURSELF

*"And let us not grow weary in doing good, for in due season we shall reap, if we do not give up."*
*Galatians 6:9 (MEV)*

One of the most frustrating things in preparation is not seeing the results of the work we've put in. As a result, many give up on their goals and dreams. The issue with this is that we could be right around the corner from a breakthrough, but never know it because we stopped walking. You have to remind yourself that your preparation is not just about reaching a destination. You have to enjoy the process of getting to that destination. Many of us grow impatient with ourselves, not because we aren't producing, but because we are viewing our results from the wrong perspective. As you prepare, allow moments where you stop and celebrate the small victories. Take time to reminisce and review the lessons you've learned.

In addition to this, we must learn how to take small breaks without quitting. For some visionaries, when you begin working on something, it's hard to stop. You go hard on the project night and day, sometimes forgetting other responsibilities like taking care of yourself, spending time with family, and serving others. Understand that working night and day on something will not make the reward come faster. Somethings just require time and patience before you see the desired fruit.

Just as when you work out you take a break between reps, remember to take small breaks between your work. Taking small breaks will allow you to:

- Stay fresh and alert.
- Have moments to appreciate all you've accomplished.
- Review lessons you've learn and check your level of operation for proof of application of those lessons.
- Fight against burn out.
- Get new and fresh ideas.

All in all, you must remember to pace yourself throughout this process. The brands, businesses, and organizations you admire weren't built overnight. They required consistency and time. The scripture focus for today reminds us not to get weary in well doing. Our reward will come in due season. We must stay faithful to the process. We have to give ourselves the space to grow and become the person who can sustain the altitude of where God desires to take us! **Let's Pray!**

*God,*

*As I continue to stretch my faith in preparing for what I do not see, give me the spirit of resilience. For I know that no matter what difficult situation comes my way, you are still in control. I will continue to have complete confidence in you. I claim victory over every area of my life: finances, family, relationships, careers, living situations, the control of my mindset, & in advancing my faith walk in you! I have planted blessed seeds into the fertile ground, and any day now, my harvest is coming! I know you did not bring me this far just to go this far! I will not give up! Thank you, God, for being my strength! In Jesus' name, Amen!*

DAY TWENTY

# DELAY IS NOT
# DENIAL

*"Because you know that the testing of your faith produces perseverance. Let perseverance finish its work so that you may be mature and complete, not lacking anything." James 1:3-4 (NIV)*

'll never forget the moment I got the call that my nephew Xavier Jr. was about to be born. I dropped everything and ran to be with my godbrother and godsister, Xavier Sr. and Kim. When we got to the hospital, the doctors checked Kim and sent her back home to wait to have the baby. We were all very confused. It took maybe an entire week before Xavier Jr. was born. At that moment, I learned a valuable lesson.

Even though Xavier Jr's birth was delayed, it was not denied. Yes, we were all prepared for his arrival, but there was a process that had to be complete before Xavier Jr could be born. If he had been born too soon, he could have been premature and would have spent his first moments in a NICU instead of being with his parents.

As we prepare, we must remember that just because something is being delayed, does not mean that your access to that thing has been denied. Even though you may feel as if you are ready for it, it may not be ready for you. Your goals and visions must spend the necessary time in the womb so that once they are birthed, they are complete and lacking nothing. Our impatience could lead to us releasing something that has not been well thought out or well developed. We have to begin to view delay as a protection of what we have been working on. God is all-knowing. Because His desire is for us to be successful, He will delay some things until they are ready, or until we are ready for them. Just take a moment and think about the many things you have desired. Looking back, I'm sure you realize that if you had gotten it when you wanted it, you could have potentially ruined it.

In your season of preparation, don't allow delay to dampen your drive. Keep working at what God has spoken to you about, knowing that when the time is right, everything will come to pass. In the meantime, you must continue to prepare for what you may not see, but you know is on the way! **Let's Pray!**

*Father God,*

*I thank you for your word! No matter what obstacle I encounter as I grow through life, I have total assurance in you! You have given me supernatural strength and a grace to continue on in the darkest of days. I know that because I have given myself to you, I have to fight hard to keep myself holy in your sight. Lord, you have given me the victory before and I am confident that you can and will do it again. I will do everything you have called me to do. I will never give up on working for you. Thank you, God, your power! In Jesus' name, Amen.*

DAY TWENTY-ONE

# PERSPECTIVE, POSITION
## &
# PRASIE

*"Do you see a man skillful in his work? He will stand before kings; he will not stand before obscure men."*
Proverbs 22:29 (ESV)

As we continue to go higher and higher in the things God has assigned us to do, we must remember to maintain a spirit of excellence. Sometimes, once we've experienced certain accomplishments, we can find ourselves getting lazy, or not feeling as though we have to do as much. The same work it took for us to get to certain levels is the same work that will be required of us to stay on those levels. So, how do we ensure that we continue to operate in excellence no matter how high God may take us? We constantly assess our perspective, position, and our praise.

**Perspective**

Our perspective is how we view things. As we mature, our perspective of life, the people around us, our goals, and our future changes. There are many things that factor into a changed perspective. For instance, when you were younger, you probably wanted to be a doctor, lawyer, or even a cashier at Walmart. However, after you matured and realized your gifts, talents, and interests, your perspective of your future changed. As we go from level to level, we must make sure that our perspective adjusts accordingly. Don't be afraid to rework your goals and plans according to what you've learned about yourself, and what God has called you to do. The reason many people get stuck, stagnant, or feel unfulfilled is that they never changed their perspective. A changed perspective not only directs you to what you should be doing, but it also enhances how you do what you do. A renewed perspective shows growth and maturity. Anything breathing should constantly be growing and maturing. To ensure that you are always growing, be sure to review your perspective of yourself and your goals constantly.

**Position**

As we elevate, so should the things we position ourselves around. It is important to position ourselves closely to the things we desire. This repositioning could mean different circles of friends, different opportunities, or visiting different places. It is very easy to become comfortable with familiarity. Understand that staying comfortable and positioning yourself around what you have always known is the quickest way to find yourself stagnant. As you go higher, you have to constantly assess the people you hang out with, the places you go, and the things you do. Are your friends conducive for where you want to go next? Are the places you frequently visit pushing you towards where you desire to be? If not, it may be time to reposition yourself for excellence.

**Praise**

It's easy to praise God for everything He has already done, but can you give Him praise for what's on the way? Understand that praise isn't contingent upon what we can see, praise is contingent upon who we know God is. As you prepare every other place in your life for elevation, you must also make sure your praise fits where you are headed. Praise has a way of encouraging us, uplifting us, and pushing us to keep going. The next time you are in a stressful situation, I dare you to give God praise! Your situation may not change immediately, but your attitude will do a complete 360! Every level will come with its trials, troubles, and tests. There's no way around it. One way you can ensure that you will make it through all the hell thrown your way is that you maintain a spirit of praise.

Well, we've come to the final day of our preparation, but your preparation shouldn't end here! If you need to go back over certain days, do that! Continue to intentionally prepare for where God desires to take you! My prayer is that over the last 21 days, you have gained insight about where God is taking you, and that you have been encouraged to prepare even though you don't have all of the details. Work hard, take breaks, and above all else, keep your faith up! **Let's Pray!**

*Father God,*
*I praise you for I know you are perfect in all your ways. Because excellence is a part of your DNA, you demand that I, as your child, live and operate with a spirit of excellence. Lord, help me to shift my perspective, position, and praise to match where you are taking me*

*in this new season. As you continue to do a new thing within me, I will take my praise to a new level. My praise will strive to reach your perfection. My trust in you will lead me to the place you have set aside for me. In Jesus' name, Amen.*

# STAY CONNECTED!

Thank you for purchasing 21 Days of Preparation. Adrian would like to connect with you!

Below are a few ways you can stay up-to-date on with Adrian's speaking engagements, new book releases, conferences, and more!

WEBSITE www.adriandavisnow.org

FACEBOOK Adrian Davis

INSTAGRAM adriandavisnow

EMAIL adm@allnationshsv.org

Made in the USA
Columbia, SC
31 July 2017